PRAISE FOR JACKIE SMITH, JR.

All too often, we come to church but, our lives are never really changed. There is power in the name of Jesus. But, there is a transformation in the Glory. But, HOW do we access it? How do we CONSISTENTLY tap into the power of His Presence?

As Lead Worshippers and Minstrels, we are commissioned to take the people of God into the Holy of Holies... the place where God's Glory resides.

This handbook contains over 30 years of experience and wisdom in attaining the Glory of God through Praise and Worship.

I pray that you are blessed and that your worship experience is increased by what God has given me to write.

ESTABLISHING GLORY

ESTABLISHING GLORY

The Praise and Worship Handbook

JACKIE SMITH, JR.

Copyright © 2019 J Merrill Publishing, Inc.

All rights reserved. No part of this publication may be reproduced, distributed, or transmitted in any form or by any means, including photocopying, recording, or other electronic or mechanical methods, without the prior written permission of the publisher, except in the case of brief quotations embodied in critical reviews and certain other noncommercial uses permitted by copyright law. For permission requests, write to the publisher, addressed "Attention: Permissions Coordinator," at the address below.

ISBN: 978-1-950719-02-0 (Hardback)
ISBN: 978-1-950719-00-6 (Paperback)
ISBN: 978-1-950719-01-3 (eBook)

Library of Congress Control Number: 2019904126

Any references to historical events, real people, or real places are used fictitiously. Names, characters, and places are products of the author's imagination.

Second printing edition 2019.

J Merrill Publishing, Inc.
434 Hillpine Drive
Columbus, OH 43207
www.JMerrill.pub

This book is dedicated to the woman who showed me how to stand firm in my convictions, learn from every situation, and see God in the midst of it all: my mother, Permelia Ann Smith.

CONTENTS

Preface   xi

1. WHAT DOES IT MEAN TO BE A LEAD WORSHIPPER?   1
2. SKILLED WORKER   7
   For the singers...   12
   For the musicians...   15
3. PASTORAL RELATIONSHIP   21
4. THE SOUND OF THE HOUSE   31
   The Priestly Church   34
   The Prophetic Church   36
   The Apostolic Church   38
5. TABERNACLE WORSHIP   45
   Outer Court   48
   Inner Court   51
   Holy of Holies   55
6. THEMATIC WORSHIP - ECHOES OF THE HOUSE   59

7. COLLABORATIVE WORSHIP - THE HEART OF THE LEAD WORSHIPPERS	63
8. THE FLOW - HEART OF GOD	69
9. PRACTICING HIS PRESENCE	73
10. THE NEXT LEVEL OF PRAISE AND WORSHIP... THE GLORY	79
Acknowledgments	89
About the Author	91

PREFACE

Before I type a single word about how to be the most significant worship leader, the most fantastic minstrel, or a phenomenal psalmist, let's address some pertinent and sobering questions.

I've been a Minister of Music, Director of Worship and Arts, Musical Director, Worship Leader, and a myriad of other "titles" in the church for over 30 years. But contrary to popular belief, none of these titles mean a thing if you can't honestly answer "Yes" to the questions later in this chapter. Otherwise, this complete manual will be just another book

PREFACE

added to the collection gathering dust next to Jakes, Bevere, and Price.

Some are already wondering, "Why did this dude start this book with such a serious tone?" So, here's the answer, and it's simple: Praise and Worship is serious.

Over the years, we've glamorized the positions. People want to sing on a stage or perform live streamed on the internet, with millions of views and thousands of followers, world-renowned, and let's not forget, paid. But Luke 12:48 (MSG) says plainly: *"Great gifts mean great responsibilities; greater gifts, greater responsibilities!"*

The first question to ask yourself is, "Are you ready for the responsibility?"

In this manual, we will discuss the responsibility and the preparation needed to fulfill this formidable task of praise and worship.

Secondly, "Are you equipped?"

As a musician/singer, do you practice your craft? Are you skillful? How much time are you currently spending on bettering yourself?

Finally, "Are you committed?"

PREFACE

I may have just lost half of my potential readers with this one. But it is what it is. We need to be committed to the task. Every gathering isn't going to be a stellar performance. There will be some less-than-stellar "YouTube" moments or failures, some that may make you laugh, and quite a few that may make you cringe and cry. There may even be some WorldStar moments (and we pray that there won't be). But the reality is that we must be committed to the task.

I'm not one to linger, so let's jump right in.

1
WHAT DOES IT MEAN TO BE A LEAD WORSHIPPER?

This manual is not designed to boost your ego or make you into something you're not intended to be. As with stereo instructions, some concepts may be stated plainly, but the real meaning can be missed.

Praise and worship aren't just about the worship team being called at the beginning of service, singing a few songs, making everyone jump for a spell, and returning to their seats after "having a good time."

Nor is it about singing the latest and greatest Top 40 "church" songs or seeing how many runs you can accomplish vocally or instrumentally.

It is about getting into the presence of Almighty God and presenting an offering to Him that will be accepted while leading the congregation into that same place. We aren't "worship leavers" but "worship leaders."

Worship leaders are those who have prepared themselves in song and spirit. They have a relationship with God outside of the four walls of the church, and they are at the helm of the ship called worship.

Simply put, "You can't take others somewhere you haven't been."

Worship is a lifestyle. It isn't like being on a crash diet to drop a bunch of pounds to fit into a specific dress or suit. It is continual. It is every day. It is nonstop. We eat, live, and breathe worship.

But wait. I am not saying that you need to be a super Christian (one who speaks in KJV, has never sinned, and every third phrase is, "the Lord told me to tell you...." No, no, no. A difference must occur in you to manifest the purpose God wants to flow *through* you.

Being a worshipper is not a solo venture. Check out 1 Chronicles 25. Did you know that when David selected the musicians, there were 288 chosen (with their families)? And *"They were well-trained in the sacred music, all of them masters"* (1 Chronicles 25:7, MSG).

A part of the responsibility isn't just leading the church congregation. You also must lead your home.

As I write this, I am reflecting on my childhood. My father was (and still is) a Minister of Music. My mother was a choir director and a songwriter. So, music was always in the house. We went to every service, practice, and performance. Even family gatherings would end up with everyone around that upright piano, singing songs and praising God. But you may be surprised that my parents never forced us to make music.

We didn't *make* music; we *were* music, and we were always learning to focus on the purpose of the music in us. So that separated us from the many whose worship is casual.

Purpose doesn't just jump out at you and -

BAM - you've arrived. Discovering the potential of your purpose is a lifelong journey.

When my brother was consecrated as an infant, the pastor spoke a special blessing over his hands. He has been a musician since he was big enough to hold two spoons and beat on the table. Others have had to learn what their purpose is: aggressively. His was thrust upon him at birth.

God has a purpose for each of us.

The key is finding out what it is and learning how to walk in it. The only way you will honestly find your purpose is to seek God more and more deeply. Jeremiah 29:11 (NIV) says, *"For I know the plans I have for you...."*

Establishing a relationship with God sets you on course for realizing your purpose. Maintaining a relationship with Him *keeps* you on the path.

So, how do we establish and maintain a relationship with God?

"Prayer, fasting, and study." It's just that simple.

Each day of being a worshipper should begin and end with God. God should fill every moment. Again, how can you lead people into a place you haven't gone?

Unfortunately, most congregants only think about God when they are in the worship service. Still, many think about what they will do after service while sitting there. We must break past all that "stuff" and help them enter His presence; if we don't, we've failed.

Yes, we've failed. It wouldn't be the congregations' fault if the praise and worship bombed. It isn't the musicians' fault because they forgot how to play the verse. It would not be the singers' fault if they didn't know the vamp. We failed as *worship leaders* to lead the people into God's presence. It is *our* fault!

Praise and worship aren't just a filler in service until the announcements and offerings are done. Preparing people's hearts and minds to receive God's spoken Word is vital. Almost half of us would miss the message if every service started with the preacher, not just because we arrived late but because our minds weren't focused on Jesus yet.

The Word of God is our living bread. You can't just open the oven and grab the rolls.

You'd burn yourself and wouldn't want another piece. The table must be prepared. The table is your heart. Once your heart is ready, receiving the bread of life is easy and beneficial.

So, as lead worshippers, we are helping to set the table by creating an atmosphere that God will saturate. This leaves us in a place ready to receive.

We have a tremendous responsibility, starting with *prayer, fasting,* and *study*.

2

SKILLED WORKER

Worship leaders must become skilled in their craft.

All too often, we live by Psalm 100:1 (KJV), "*Make a joyful noise unto the Lord, all ye lands.*" But the problem with this is that making a "joyful noise" needs to become a mindset.

We are reminded in Proverbs 23:7, "*For as he thinketh in his heart, so is he.*"

We set ourselves up for mediocrity when God wants better. And not just better, He wants the *best*. But settling to be "joyful noisers" opens us up to a spirit of slothfulness.

When we relegate ourselves to being "joyful noisers," not only do we not study the music, but often we haven't even *listened* to it before practice. We come to practice with our minds all over the place. We are unfocused. Teaching a new song becomes impossible, and reviewing old songs is a strain. We present the songs to God before the congregation half-heartedly. Then, we wonder why the song (s) didn't go over and the people didn't "get with us."

Instead of making a joyful noise, we should have a mindset of *perfected praise*. Matthew 21:16 (NKJV) clarifies that even *"out of the mouth of babes and nursing infants, you have perfected praise."*

What is 'perfected praise,' and what does it have to do with being a skilled worker? The simple answer is that perfected praise comes from the heart. It's true worship.

One of my favorite worship songs is "The Anthem" by Planet Shakers. One of my worship team leaders suggested this song. When I first heard it, it was a "nice song." Being in an "Apostolic" house (more to come on that), the song matched the sound of the house. So, we started to learn it. As I began playing this song at home, the Spirit of the Lord consumed me, and I couldn't stop playing it. I played and played. Time was no longer a factor. And God Himself was in the studio with me. When I finally ended my practice time, almost two hours had passed, and I had only practiced this ONE song!

My spirit connected with this song. So, whenever this song is presented, it immediately connects with me, and what is *in* me naturally comes *out*.

And that's perfected praise.

The key here is we must open ourselves up, eat the whole fruit, and allow it to nourish us spiritually. You see, perfected praise is *ministry*. So, just as the preacher prepares their mind, body, and spirit to preach, the same applies to the worshipper. The difference here is that the preacher is preparing to minister to the congregation, but the worshipper is preparing to minister to God.

I remember when my younger brother was growing up. His appetite for music was insatiable. I've never seen anything like it. He would wake up and begin practicing on the piano/keyboard. He would take breaks only when he had no choice. Then, he'd go right back to practicing. Sometimes, he would play for 8-10 hours each day. And he did it because that was his passion and desire. That's what naturally came out of him: a need to improve his musical skills. No wonder he has "perfect pitch;" he can teach 5- & 6-part harmonies on the fly. He is continually sought after. Why? Because he worked his craft and honed his skills.

Compared to my brother, the 2-3 hours I would practice seemed like nothing. But everyone has their purpose, calling, and destiny. We should never compare ourselves to others because we don't know what God intends for them versus what He plans for us. What is important is that we perfect what God has given us individually.

And, as we continue perfecting our gifts, the praise comes more naturally. So, Matthew 11:29-30 KJV says, *"Take my yoke upon you, and learn of me; for I am meek and lowly in heart: and ye shall find rest unto your souls. For my yoke is easy, and my burden is light."*

In this example, the yoke is the praise, and the burden is the practice. When we begin this journey of perfected praise, it may seem impossible.

I remember when the worship completely sucked three Sundays in a row. The band was off. The singers sang the wrong words and parts. The people were disengaged. The pastor had to rescue the service again. But as you continue to fight past the distractions of everyday life, disappointments, and troubles and learn how to get into that place of praise, the praise (the yoke) becomes easy. The more you do it in your personal practice (the burden), the lighter it becomes. To create perfected praise corporately, we must perfect our praise individually.

Again, how can you take people to a place you don't go to?

Another thing must be addressed: when it comes to being a skillful worker, what exactly are we perfecting?

JACKIE SMITH, JR.

FOR THE SINGERS...

To be clear, praying, fasting, living a Godly life, and seeking the Kingdom have to be a given.

- Learn the music.

The singer's version of learning the music is knowing the words and your part. Missing either of these two can destroy the flow of worship.

- Spend time singing to God.

Occasionally, during worship service, a "River" of the Spirit's presence draws the congregation to sing to the Lord. People will sing things like, "Lord, you are good," "Lord, we worship You," and "We extol you, God." This is good, but our worship should be even more in-depth as lead worshippers. And we increase our depth in spiritual songs by singing to God privately.

Of course, you may need help to start. So,

how about we sing His Word? There's an entire book of songs called Psalms. Sing your favorite scriptures. While studying the Word, sing what God reveals to you. The more you do this, the easier it becomes when the service calls for it.

- Make the songs personal.

Search each song as it relates to the Bible and apply your OWN testimony. There's nothing more BORING than hearing people sing the notes with no character or feeling. On the other side, there's nothing more disengaging than hearing someone run a vocal marathon throughout an entire song without any connection to what they're singing.

When we search out a song in the Bible, we connect that song to God. But we may need another song if we can't compare that song to the Word. So, what is the purpose of singing a song that doesn't connect with Yeshua?

After we've connected that song to Him, we need to apply our testimony to that song.

Our focus here is on the congregation. We are to lead the listener to the Father. So, how much we are engaged and connected or disengaged with and disconnected from a song, the listener will follow suit. Unfortunately, people focus on the negative or what's most like them. So, if I'm singing, "God, You Reign forever, and I worship you," and I'm disconnected from the song, the listener will often be detached from the music.

They are following your lead. And this doesn't just happen with solos. It happens with devotional and worship teams, quartets, and choirs.

By nature, people seek what's most like them. That's why it's so important to be engaged in the music and have a relationship with God. If everyone on stage is connected and engaged, then the people more naturally follow our lead.

FOR THE MUSICIANS...

As with singers, your spirit man must be fed and strengthened daily. There's no excuse for anyone not praying, fasting, seeking Kingdom things, and living Godly.

- Learn the music.

Drummers, you should know not only the music's rhythms and the changes needed throughout the song (s), but you should also know and be able to control the tempo, or speed, of the song. Keyboardists naturally play songs differently than it's supposed to. So, the drummers keep the original rhythm locked down.

Keyboardists and guitarists should know the chords, progressions, and phrases within a song and the song in multiple keys. The reason is simple. What happens when the pastor requests a song that Sister Jane leads, but she is recovering from a cold and can't hit that high C? We, as musicians, need to adjust the song to accommodate the voices. Also, many songwriters write for specific groups or choirs. Some worship teams cannot perform all the vocal acrobatics or reach all the notes in a Hezekiah Walker song. So, we change the key to one that is comfortable for them.

- Practice in every key

If my 'favorite' key is C, I will practice in C whenever I sit down at the keyboard. But not every song is in the key of C. What happens when Bro. John sings in the key of G? I just heard a group of musicians say, "Just hit the transpose button!" No way. That's just *lazy*.

The better question is, what happens when you are forced to play the piano or an "old-school" Hammond organ? There is no transpose button and forcing people to sing in your "comfort keys" is wrong. Plus, some people won't move from the key they're singing in. So, will you then blame the singer for not adjusting to your key? Or will you continue playing in the wrong key for the whole song? We need to practice in EVERY key; it's as simple as that.

- Respect your instrument

This one should have been first. When you respect your instrument, you spend time with it. I can't even number the times I've spoken with musicians who don't practice. They will listen to the music once or twice. Then, try to perform that music on Sunday morning. Or worse, they spend the choir/worship team's practice time learning the songs while the singers are supposed to be cleaning up their parts. It's a travesty. Not only are you disrespecting your instrument and your craft, but you are also disrespecting the singers, the songwriter, the listeners, and ultimately, God. You're putting your talent under a rock. And if you remember, the fellow who failed to grow and strengthen the gift he had been given was called a "wicked and slothful servant" (Jesus' words, not mine).

- Know your role.

The role of the musician is to accompany the singer (s). I'm going to reveal a secret. Did you know that musicians have a more prominent voice than singers? Well, they do. That's why we have microphones for the SINGERS. Their voices must be amplified to clarify the words and parts and lessen the strain on the singers' voices. But microphones were NOT created so the voices could be heard over the music. If the voices are at 10, the music should be at 7. But all too often, the music is on 10 with the singers, and the musicians still ask for more volume because they "can't hear themselves." The answer is NOT louder music. It's quite the opposite.

The answer is bringing the music down. The volume on your keyboard should *never* be all the way up while there are singers at the mic. Have we considered what happens to the listener during these volume battles on stage?

Therefore, during our practices, things like a soundcheck, communicating the levels on each song, and having a sound engineer present at practices are essential. Don't forget; the Kingdom's goal is for the message to be heard, and the music enhances the message, not drown it out.

3

PASTORAL RELATIONSHIP

The first step in building the pastoral relationship is *respect*. Over the years, I have played with some of the most amazing pastors. Please note that I played "with" these pastors. I did not play "for" them.

As musicians, we must understand our role within the ministry. We indeed enhance the worship experience. We take charge of and create an atmosphere for the glory of God. And we certainly make going to church more enjoyable for the congregants. But our role is to accompany the pastor.

To accompany means to "go somewhere with (someone) as a companion or escort;" it also means to "be present or occur at the same time as (something else)."

My question is: How can you go somewhere with someone, and you don't know where they're going? To understand where pastors are going, you must spend time with them. First, you need to learn about who they are. Then you need to know their ministry goals and overall goals in life. Finally, you need to "date" your pastor (not literally, figuratively).

Once it's determined where we're going, we will know whether we are headed in the same direction. Let's not forget that we are traveling together. If you're going one way and the pastor is going another way, there will be problems. It is best to part ways when this happens, just as Abram and Lot did.

But all too often, we get wrapped up in the "business" of the church. When there's a need, churches are posting positions, using social media to search for musicians, and even using referral services to look for candidates

ESTABLISHING GLORY

for these openings. Musicians then send in their resumes, credentials, referrals, etc. The church will then schedule interviews with the prospects, and the hiring process continues.

Don't get me wrong; I don't disagree with the process of weeding out folks. Some people just aren't qualified to be salaried musicians. But where do we draw the line between being a hireling (John 10:12-13) and being a *"laborer worthy of his hire"* (1 Timothy 5:18)?

The difference between a hireling and a laborer is the expectation. Of course, the pastor respects the musicians and their gifts or talents in both cases. But there is a difference in the level of expectation that needs to focus beyond the skills and even more on the heart for the ministry the musician brings to the relationship.

I have known musicians who play for three or more services on Sunday mornings. While sitting on the organ in church number one, they watch the clock because they must leave by 8:15 a.m. to get to the next church service, which starts at 9:00 a.m. Once they reach church number two, they watch the clock because they must leave by 10:00 am for the next church service, which starts at 10:30 am. And the cycle goes on and on.

Some churches will even delay their service because the musician is running late from his other church. The only common denominator between these churches is that they pay this musician. If they didn't pay him, then he wouldn't come. But sad to say, the church knows that if they can't pay him, for whatever reason, he won't be there.

This hireling doesn't care for the sheep, the ministry, the pastoral vision, or anything other than the money. And when everyone knows this, then expectations are established.

When the pastor and musician labor together, the expectations are different. Because they understand co-laboring, the pastor can ask that the musician not only come to rehearsals and services but also attend Bible study, where there is no music and no additional pay. The kicker is that the laborer will come and will not complain. Why? Because the musician accompanies the pastor, the more time they spend together, the tighter the bond between them, and the further they can take the ministry.

Earlier, I stated that the pastor and musician should 'date' one another. Well, after dating comes the union. There's nothing more potent than a pastor and musician who walk together in unity.

I once played with a pastor for six months without discussing getting a salary or compensation. I came to services and rehearsals 15-30 minutes early every time. I started attending Bible study. And the pastor and I met weekly to discuss the direction of the music department and other ministry items. This was an actual labor of love.

During this time, the pastor chose all the music. This was different for me, but it was cool; that was one less thing I had to do (or so I thought).

What happened is I learned who my pastor was, what his expectations were, where I fit into the ministry, when I was needed in the various areas of ministry (not just music-related), how to respond and react to different scenarios, and why I, as an individual and not just a musician, should be a part of this ministry. As a result, he and I became friends. I would compare our relationship with Jonathan and David. There IS nothing that will come between the love that we have for each other.

Then, one day after a Sunday service, the church secretary called me into the office. She said the pastor wanted to ensure that I was taken care of, and she had a check for me. So, my commitment to the ministry was established long before I ever talked about or received any money.

Proverbs 18:16 (AMP) says, *"A man's gift [given in love or courtesy] makes room for him and brings him before great men."* We can miss out on the greater blessing by "charging" for our services. We miss out on the relationship and the covenant partnership.

That is what the pastoral relationship is about. It's a covenant. And we walk in agreement, speak the same thing, walk the same way, and move through ministry in lockstep. But, once that happens, we run into the power of this union and the experience of "delegated authority" from a Divine perspective. In the spirit realm, God delegated His authority to the pastor to speak on His behalf. The same holds true for the pastor and the lead worshipper. Pastors transfer their power to the lead worshipper to speak on their behalf, just as God gives the pastors His authority. Unfortunately, the problem with many churches is that this authority is too often mishandled, abused, and sometimes wielded like a child playing with his toys.

This covenant can be volatile because we don't truly understand what we're dealing with or the ramifications of the worship team and the individuals surrounding us.

The most powerful example of this bond can be seen between God and Lucifer. We can imagine God, as the Pastor, sets Lucifer up as Minister of Music. They worked very well together for some time. Unfortunately, Lucifer got beside himself and felt he needed a bigger office than the Pastor. He felt everyone was coming to the service to hear him do his thing. He felt like the Pastor should retire so that he could take over the church. Why? Because he had a voice just like the Pastor did.

So, like many pastors have to do today, God had to fire his Minister of Music. I know He fired Lucifer because Luke 10:18 (AMP) says, "I watched Satan fall from heaven like [a flash of] lightning." God had to put him out. And just like today's churches, all those who followed the Minister of Music went with him. So, a *third* of the church fell when they followed the wrong leader.

We need to know our roles.

This point must be established during the initial phases of building the pastoral relationship. Then, as we become more intimate with our leader, we must understand and navigate these fixed boundaries. The church secretary gave one of the most influential pieces of advice. She said, "You need to know when you're dealing with the Bishop and when you're dealing with 'James' because they are two different people." And that is true.

As musicians, we can be cool. We can laugh and talk. We can even be friends. But don't ever get casual and treat God's gifts as "common." Ephesians 4:11 (NLT) says, *"Now these are the gifts Christ gave to the church: the apostles, the prophets, the evangelists, and the pastors and teachers."* When we get casual about the gifts, we devalue, diminish, and dilute the purpose of those gifts.

So, when we first started serving, the pastors could say nothing wrong. They were one of the most profound blessings God ever gave the church. They were the greatest!

But as time passes, we cannot help but see Noah in his nakedness. We may be there when Moses smites the rock instead of speaking to it as God wanted.

"Man, the pastor is just rambling again." "That's the same message that he preached last week." "Doesn't he have any fresh revelations?" "I can preach better than that." Sound familiar? It's the same thing Lucifer said when he was Minister of Music.

We are out of alignment with the pastor.

When we know our roles, the established boundaries within our pastoral-musician union become clear. As the musician, I am here to do a job: to lead the music department into a mindset of bringing God's glory to every event we're involved in. We are the Cherubim who carry the Glory of God. Since we know our role, we aren't offended when only the pastor is invited to a special dinner after service while we still need to break down the equipment. Even though I'm in the room with the pastor, I don't need to be "in" on every conversation. We understand that *every* word spoken behind closed doors is spoken in confidence. We don't "uncover" our leaders, leaving them exposed.

We are partners. We have our own identities, but we speak from the same script. We walk the same paths. Our destinies are intertwined. And most importantly, God is guiding us, both of us.

The most successful and impactful ministries have strong pastoral and lead worshipper relationships. God guides ministries through these single-minded pairs and groups.

4
THE SOUND OF THE HOUSE

This chapter expresses the importance of attending Bible Class, a truth inspired by a lesson taught by my former pastor, Apostle Brian Keith Williams.

Before we can address the "Sound of the House," we need to understand what "type" of a house that church is. It's funny because I've gone into churches and felt like I stepped into a time warp. I walked in and was transported back into the 1960s. They had an organ and drums, but no one to play them. However, they had tambourines and a solid foot stomp.

And they *had church*!

Then, again, I've stepped into what we call Mega-Churches. They had closed-circuit televisions scattered throughout the building, the big screens hanging in the sanctuary. The band was filled with accomplished musicians, and the music was so tight that it sounded like a recording.

And they enjoyed the Lord.

In these two examples, the sound was incredibly different. But the spirit was the same. How can this be? It's simple. The Spirit of God doesn't change. He is the same wherever you go. The only difference is the presentation of God.

How we present God matters; because we, as people, are different. And when we genuinely break it down, every church falls into one of three categories: Priestly, Prophetic, or Apostolic.

Many would say they know their church is Apostolic because it's written on the sign out front. Churches in this category are not affiliated with any particular doctrine. And many Apostolic churches flow in different styles. These types of churches are a significant subject on their own, But I'll briefly talk about each one now.

JACKIE SMITH, JR.

THE PRIESTLY CHURCH

This church flows from a perspective of *Truth*. The foundation is solidly based on tradition, the King James way, and the teaching speaks of where God *was* and what Jesus has done.

I grew up in a Priestly Church. We had services, or church events, 6-7 days a week. On Sundays, we arrived at 9:30 a.m. for Sunday School and wouldn't leave until 9:00 p.m. because we had services scheduled throughout the *entire* day.

We were taught holiness or hell. The Word of God is the "end all—be all" of any matter. So, we don't argue about the Word of God.

We devote our lives to studying the Word of God. And we live our lives according to the scripture.

The key here is that we focused on *loving Jesus* and *being with God*.

How does that affect the worship?

These churches are considered "old school." There was always a printed program with the "Order of Service." There was little deviation from that order. The song list will contain.... Wait, there were no song lists for the worship. There were plenty of choruses, hymns, and songs from yesteryear; they may have a choir or two, and they may still have a devotional service where the congregation randomly leads the songs.

The real focus of the worship is not worship itself. The actual center is on the Word and what comes after the worship. Therefore, congregational involvement during worship was expected but not encouraged.

We went from one song to the next. Unless God "took over."

As I stated earlier, I grew up in this type of church. I don't know where I would be had it not been for the teaching at this church. We all need a foundation.

JACKIE SMITH, JR.

THE PROPHETIC CHURCH

This church flows in the *Spirit of Truth*. The approach is progressive. King James is the fallback, but you're more likely to see NIV, NLT, or even the Message bible being used. The teaching speaks of where God *is*.

I played with a Prophetic Church. This ministry moved in the revelation of God's Word. It's one thing to know God's Word, but another to see how it applies to your life today. The same scripture that has been read over and over now has a new understanding. The Word became a living and breathing part of my life.

The key here is to focus on *hearing Jesus* and *moving with God*.

How does that affect the worship?

There is more preparation for worship. There is a printed program, but the "service is subject to change." There is a worship team that is dedicated to worship, not only in singing but in prayer and fasting. Worship isn't just a steppingstone to God's spoken Word. The song list will include Top 40 music from several genres (Gospel, CCM, etc.). Congregational involvement is encouraged but not expected.

The proper focus here is setting the atmosphere or preparing the way for the Lord. It's not uncommon for the worship service to go long, and the placement/timing of the sermon change because of the atmosphere that has been set.

We pause between songs to allow the message to *simmer*.

I loved being in this environment. Of course, there is always a plan, but you must be on your toes.

JACKIE SMITH, JR.

THE APOSTOLIC CHURCH

This church flows in *Spirit and Truth*. The approach is restorative. King James is used, but so is the Amplified. The teaching is about where God *will be*.

As members of an Apostolic Church, we move in the revelation of God's Word and the declaration of things to come. We don't just speak of where Jesus was and where He is, but we walk in the authority of God and declare the next step— "in the name of Jesus Christ, rise up and walk!"

We move into the "I AM." "I am the head and not the tail." "I am more than a conqueror," "I may be going thru the valley, but I am healed."

The key here is to focus on *being like Jesus* and *governing with God*. The stance is positional instead of conditional, sitting at the right hand of the Father, not simply focusing on our current situation.

I must be honest; as I started this section, I felt a quickening in my spirit. I could preach this. But I'll refrain. I must pause for a 'praise break.'

Ok... I'm back.

How does this affect the worship?

Simple. It becomes relational. Worship is a part of the Word. They are no longer separate parts of worship. To prepare for the worship, the preacher and the praiser fast, pray, and communicate with each other. The song list may include full hymns, i.e., all the verses, top 40 from multiple genres, songs from yesteryear, and spontaneous worship songs of the Lord. The service is focused on *one* message, one central truth, and the printed program is apt to be discarded.

We may arrive for the service, and the order is changed entirely. Instead of beginning the service in worship and ending with the Word, the Word may come first. The worship may be so engulfed in the Spirit of God that the preacher may join the worship and end the worship with an altar appeal.

Spontaneous worship is liable to break out at any moment.

I love this environment because it's always charged. An unmistakable feeling of unity allows more freedom for the Spirit of God.

So, why go through all these diverse types of churches when this chapter is called "The Sound of the House?"

Everyone has a sound that they align with spiritually. God has blessed me to experience these different churches, glean from them, and share with you the differences. But when it came to the church I felt aligned with, there was a leap in my spirit.

The problem is that musicians often don't follow the leading of the Lord when selecting a church to play with. Instead, they are playing for a church to get paid. But what happens to your soul, your ministry, and your calling?

The reason that I established the types of churches is so that you could relate to the church that you align with. The size of the church is immaterial. I've played at churches with less than 20 people and churches with over 10,000 people. It honestly doesn't matter how many people are in the congregation. I want you to be where God wants you.

Proverbs 18:16 says that your gift will make room for you. When you are correctly connected, you'll get paid. God will take care of you in ways that seem impossible.

Musically, each house has a requirement that needs to be met. Luke 12:48 AMP says, "From everyone to whom much has been given, much will be required; and to whom they entrusted much, of him they will ask all the more." How does this apply musically?

I've been to churches where the pastor and the congregation were okay with the musician playing every song in the key of C. Every chord progression was the same. All the runs were the same. They were even performed at the same volume.

The music selection was the same music from when granddaddy was the pastor. Nothing has changed.

You're in a Priestly house. The requirement is smaller. So, the expectations and the work match the demand. And so does the pay. I know a young man who plays for a church and is excited about the $50 they give him every Sunday. He is in the right place. His sound matches the sound of the house.

I was at a church once, and the pastor asked me to study Benny Hinn's music. He then gave me a Benny Hinn Ministries (BHM) compilation of 3 or 4 CDs. And, quite honestly, it was hard!

That music was not appealing to me. I listened and listened. I spent hours, days, and weeks absorbing this music. Then, I began to understand something.

I see the patterns in the flow of the music. I saw why Benny Hinn has such an anointing for healing and restoration. He found the path and tapped into something we weren't doing in our services. And my pastor, being a true Apostolic, wanted our worship to tap in. This new expectation required that I do more work and do work that I didn't like.

But it worked. Our worship excelled by applying what I had learned by listening to music I didn't care for. How many would have received those CDs and politely never listened to them?

Our level of work ethic will help to determine what type of church is the right fit for us. For example, if you're comfortable learning three new songs a month, you may be comfortable in a Prophetic church.

As musicians and worshippers, we must keep our ears open and attentive to what God has for the house, whatever your house may be.

You learn what is in the church by observing. Whenever I've started playing with a new house, I refrain from making song list suggestions for the first 3–6 months of my tenure. Instead, I receive recommendations from the pastor and the worship team. This way, I am learning what 'type' of pastor and 'type' of worshippers are in the house. During service, I observe the 'type' of congregation in the house. And you really can't make judgments until after at least three months.

Once we understand that *the sound of the house* reflects the *type of house* and the *type of pastor*, we can know if we are a good fit for this house long term.

Now that we've discussed the sound of the house, let's talk about the various methods used for establishing that sound.

5
TABERNACLE WORSHIP

The tabernacle, or tent of meeting, was the dwelling place of the Spirit of God. God meticulously described how it was built, its décor, how things were to be managed, the preparation before entering, and so much more.

So, my question is, if God was so purposeful regarding His dwelling place, why aren't we just as persistent when we desire His presence?

All too often, worshippers come to service without a worship clue. There is an expectation of God's presence, but there has been no preparation. No prayer, no fasting, no seeking God, and unfortunately... NO SONGS.

And we've all been there. Unfortunately, this week was busy, and I didn't have much time. But as I drove to service this morning, these songs "dropped in my spirit."

So, everyone gets in the "pre-service huddle" around someone's smartphone, scratchpad, sticky note, or back of an offering envelope, and this is what we're singing today.

The problem is that only a few often know the music, including the musicians. The rhythm is incorrect. The key is too high or too low. Oh, and let's not forget the *words*! But God is expected to show up and show out.

God doesn't dwell in confusion, which is why many churches experience a 'visitation' so infrequently.

Worship is a lifestyle. In 1 Chronicles 25:7 (NET), we find an important reference to the worship musicians: *"They and their relatives, all of them skilled and trained to make music to the LORD."* Not only was the worshipper trained and skillful, but so was their family. They lived their music!

So, *we* must follow suit. *We* must bring our best before the Lord.

One of the most effective methods for building the Worship Song List is what I call Tabernacle Worship.

Three defined parts of the Tabernacle (Outer Court, Inner Court, and Holy of Holies) make Tabernacle Worship.

JACKIE SMITH, JR.

OUTER COURT

Most people aren't prepared for the worship experience when the worship service begins. So, as worship leaders, it is our responsibility to help draw the people in and guide them into the presence of God.

In the Outer Court, this is where we sing songs *directed to the people*.

Songs like "Come on and bless the Lord with me," "Let It Rise," and "Friend of God" are all directed at the person in the pew.

These songs also help people to become more involved in worship and get them out of their seats.

We, as worship leaders, must never forget to include the congregants in the worship. Worship isn't a spectator sport. We must consciously do certain things, like singing songs that include our audience and asking them to stand. Keyword: ASK.

Be mindful not to become agitated when the audience isn't doing what you expect. Yelling at the people to stand to their feet or to sing with you isn't engaging. The people aren't robots, and it takes time for them to unload their stuff. So, walk in patience and wisdom.

One other thing about the Outer Court is simplicity and repetition.

Notice in the song examples above there are very few words, and those few words are repeated a lot. This is particularly important. It's easier for me to sing with you and unload my stuff when I don't have to read the screens.

One quick note.

What does it mean to "unload your stuff?" If we want people to be engaged in what we're doing, we must help them shift their focus. Unfortunately, focusing on worship is tough when the average person has a thousand other things on their mind. We all deal with struggles from one service to the next. Things happen on the job, at home, and sometimes, in the car on the way to service. As worshippers, we must help people "unload their stuff" and shift their focus to worshipping our Great and Mighty God.

So, keeping the Outer Court songs lively,

JACKIE SMITH, JR.

simple, and repetitive helps to move the congregant from listener or watcher to active participant. Remember, the worshipper's focus in the Outer Court is on the people.

INNER COURT

Now that we've helped the congregants unload their stuff, it's time to enter the Inner Court. This is where we sing *songs that are about God*.

Songs like "He Is Lord," "How Great Is Our God," and "Shout to the Lord" are still conversational with the congregant, but the subject is no longer about the person. We are now describing God's attributes.

The Inner Court music needs to reflect the focus of Matthew 6:9, which says, "...*Our Father, who is in heaven.*" That is the beginning of the prayer. Well, this is the same place worship needs to begin.

So, just as described in the Lord's Prayer, we start the actual worship by talking *about* God: who He is, what He is like, how great He is, how marvelous He is, etc.

The Inner Court is transitional. We are transitioning our minds from us and the stuff of this life and this world to begin focusing on God and heavenly reality. This transition isn't always smooth because we're accustomed to talking about ourselves and our stuff. It isn't natural for us to focus on someone other than ourselves.

We recently went out to eat with some friends. Unfortunately, the service at the restaurant was terrible. When we brought the service to management's attention, the manager began discussing their lousy service experiences. This is relevant because we do the same regarding God and His service. This is a real example of how misdirected and self-focused our attention can be.

This is also why keeping the music "tight" in the Inner Court is imperative. *Tight* in this respect means to keep it Godward. It's way too easy to internalize songs that speak of His attributes and mentally apply them to someone other than God. This is especially evident when it comes to Godly love. His love is undeniable, unforgettable, and unending. But when you start thinking of your girlfriend, spouse, or someone else, you are tainting the music.

During the transition into the Inner Court, musicians stick to the script. Just because the melody from Fantasy by Earth, Wind, and Fire "fits" into that song does not mean it's acceptable to play it.

I've been in services where the transition was being made into the Inner Court, and God was entering the building. The congregation was fully participating in the worship. The worship team was on one accord, and the spirit was flowing. Then, the musicians started playing "I Wish" by Carl Thomas at the center of this move.

The problem with playing secular music during worship isn't that the music is worldly. The problem is that the music is "familiar." The music no longer accompanies the worship but is now distracting because the listener is trying to figure out where they've heard that melody.

People also have memories associated with music. For example, playing "You Make Me Wanna" by Usher or "Flashlight" by Parliament during service can transport people back to a particular moment or season in their lives that can remove them mentally from the service entirely. And, once a person has disconnected from the service, there's no telling if they will reconnect and be able to receive what they need from God.

Relative to time, this portion of the worship should be more significant than the Outer Court portion. Remember, it's about transitioning our attention from ourselves to God. The Outer Court experience includes everything from the moment service begins until we move into the Inner Court of worship. So, the Outer Court is more preparatory in its structure, including scripture reading and opening prayer, whereas the Inner Court is more purposeful and transitional.

HOLY OF HOLIES

Now that we've transitioned from the Outer Court to the Inner Court, it's time to shift our focus from singing *about* God to singing songs *to* God.

Songs like "Give Me You," performed by Shana Wilson, "What a Beautiful Name," performed by Hillsong Worship, and "Trust in You" by Anthony Brown are directed to God.

This section of the worship is much more intimate. Where the Outer Court is preparatory, the Inner Court is more purposeful in its transitory state. The Holy of Holies is personal and relational.

It's easy to sing to each other about God, but it's a different story when we peel back the layers and reveal our relationship with our Lord, Savior, and Creator. So, you see, this is the Love section.

We tell HIM how much we love Him, how we feel about Him, what we think about Him, and what we will do for Him. It's ALL directed to Him and how He influences us.

JACKIE SMITH, JR.

Keep the journey in mind, and don't blow it.

One of the most significant errors in this section is shifting the focus away from God because of the nature of the songs. It is easy to slip into sensuality and carnality in our minds during worship. This shift away from God shifts the entire worship, and once the worship ends, the service is no higher than when we started in the Outer Court.

I've seen singers and musicians focus on that cutie on the second row and sing about letting 'the rivers of my worship flow to you.' Or sing about taking me 'to that secret place, where I can be with You,' and the real message of "Wrap Me in Your Arms" is lost in the singer's delivery and sometimes even sensual motions.

When effectively done, Tabernacle Worship strips down the listener by helping them get rid of all their stuff, let down their guards, and open their hearts to receive from God. But when we take advantage of the listener's vulnerabilities, we are not only doing a disservice to them but acting on the same level as Lucifer. We are taking what belongs to God and using it for our own glory and benefit. And that's what happens whenever we do things to shift the listener's focus to us instead of to God.

Psalm 22:3 KJV says, *"But thou art holy, O thou that inhabitest the praises of Israel."* The purpose of the Holy of Holies section of Tabernacle Worship is to present the praises to God because He inhabits our praise! So, as we shine the light on our Father in heaven and worship Him, He is bound by His Word to show up!

6
THEMATIC WORSHIP - ECHOES OF THE HOUSE

In 1 Corinthians 14:33 (MSG), the apostle tells us, *"When we worship the right way, God doesn't stir us up into confusion; he brings us into harmony. This goes for all the churches - no exceptions."*

This is the most appropriate scripture for Thematic Worship that I could find. Simply stated, "God doesn't dwell in confusion," and when the worship and the Word are saying different things, a genuine visitation from God can be hindered.

The premise behind Thematic Worship is to echo the messages taught in the house, which involves coordinating the pastor and the worship leader. This is especially powerful when there is a series being given.

Let's say that the series will be about the Love of God. Therefore, the music selected for the worship will have a particular and purposeful message that speaks to God's Love. i.e., "Oh How He Loves You and Me," "No Greater Love," and "Glorious Day (Living He Loved Me)."

The second part is to continue this theme after the spoken Word has ended. So, during the altar appeal or dismissal, continue worshipping with songs directly related to the last part of the message, i.e., the pastor is ending the word with a theme of "flowing in the spirit, so songs like "Let the River Flow," "Fresh Flow from Heaven," or "Flow to You" would all be appropriate to continue that message in song.

The entire service is now saturated with *one* message or theme, instead of the worship service going down one road and the pastor going down another. So, when the congregation leaves, they most likely remember what was taught. And that is the crucial part.

When the worship sets the atmosphere in a single theme, the pastor continues in that same theme; the ground of our hearts doesn't have to be re-tilled. The worship breaks the soil and plants the seed. The pastor then fertilizes and waters that seed. When the altar appeal is made, and the theme is continued further, then that seed has no choice but to SPROUT. Result: changed lives!

But again, the tricky part of Thematic Worship is the coordination between the pastor and the worship leader. This works better with ministry leaders who plan out the messages in advance. If the pastor is more 'random' in delivering the messages, then this method of worship is not the best for your service regularly. Plan to use this method during consistent times of the year, like conferences, special ceremonies, and holidays, where the theme is established and less likely to change.

7
COLLABORATIVE WORSHIP - THE HEART OF THE LEAD WORSHIPPERS

Psalm 34:3 KJV says, *"O magnify the Lord with me, and let us exalt his name together."*

One of the worst places to be, especially in worship, is alone and out on an island. As lead worshippers, sometimes we aren't connected to God. Life is happening to us: family, work, school, and many other distractions. We don't have time to pray. We haven't listened to any music. Everything comes simultaneously, and the songs must be selected for service. So, what do we do?

For many years, I would look over our

current music library and pick a few songs. Two things would happen when I did this.

1. I always seemed to lean towards songs that spoke to my issues and made *me* feel better about what I was dealing with. Or...
2. I was merely out of sync with where God indeed was. As a result, I ended up having abusive practices, lots of agitation amongst the worshippers, and the worship service bombed.

Missing the move of God is a travesty.

Missing God during worship to God is an even greater disaster because this is the time of service dedicated to Him.

Then enters Collaborative Worship.

The premise behind this type of worship is to include the rest of the lead worshippers in the song selection process. So, instead of scanning the song library for songs that jump out at me, I ask the other lead worshippers, "What song (s) has God placed in your spirit this week?" "What have you been singing in your prayer time?" or "What scriptures has God been giving you this week?"

Some of the most powerful worship services I've ever experienced have used Collaborative Worship. Why?

We must never forget that the worship team, or choir, is a sampling of the congregation. The same things the 'people' are experiencing are the same things that the worshippers are experiencing. The difference is that the worshippers should be in a better position to receive direction from God and share what He is saying.

The crazy thing is that when the people are indeed on one accord, you will see an overlap in the submitted songs, and an overwhelming theme will rise out of those songs.

For instance, after having a very trying week, the songs that I wanted to sing were "Overcome" by Jeremy Camp, the chorus "Greater is He that liveth in me," and "How Great is Our God" by Chris Tomlin. So, my focus would be on God's power and defeating the enemy. This is not a bad lineup. But the suggested songs from the lead worshippers were... "Welcome into This Place" by Bruce Ballinger, "Fill Me Up" by Will Reagan, and "I Give Myself Away" by William McDowell. The music focused on God coming in and filling our hearts. Then we are being used by Him, which is ENTIRELY different from where I was coming from.

The only 'trick' to using Collaborative Worship is where the suggestions are coming from and the order of the songs.

When my worship teams have been over ten people, I've only asked for suggestions from the lead worshippers and select band members. Very rarely have I asked for suggestions from the entire worship team. The Bible tells us in 1 Thessalonians 5:12 (KJV) to "...*know them which labour among you.*" So, we know who is spending time with God and who may be struggling like you are that week.

Setting the order of the songs can be a trial because the right music at the wrong moment can shift the service in the wrong direction. So, I will combine the previous worship methods, i.e., Tabernacle Worship or Thematic Worship. I'll present the songs to the pastor and ask them what order to offer the worship.

8

THE FLOW - HEART OF GOD

One genuinely helpful way of presenting the worship set is to allow God to flow through the music. This may sound like a simple statement, but unfortunately, many of us have let the clock determine the flow instead of God.

What I mean is that we, in today's generation, expect that everything that we experience needs to happen quickly. We live life fast and, in a hurry, so we bring that same mentality into the worship service.

I'm guilty of not wanting to spend 4-6

hours in service. So, I petitioned the pastor to shorten the worship service from 45 to 30 minutes. His response was classic: he was looking for ways to extend the worship to a full hour!

But how many churches have the clock hanging on the back wall, sitting on the first row, or even positioned underneath the podium? Why is this clock there? It reminds those in leadership that we must be out of service at a particular time. So, don't go over your allotted time.

Before going further, let me define what the 'flow' is.

When entering the 'flow' or 'spontaneous worship,' we allow the song we just sang a moment to "simmer." We often rush from one song to the next without letting the message in each song settle in the listener's heart. Instead, we abruptly switch from one message to another. We're yanking the listeners from one movement and stuffing a new move down their spiritual throats without providing time for them to digest anything.

So, the flow is that space between the

songs where there is only music, a time to allow the voice of the Lord to speak through the lead worshippers or just the flow of the music itself. Many call this "spontaneous worship" because it is not practiced or prepared. Instead, it's a shadow of the previous song (meaning that the music may be a continuation of the song). The message is usually a word of knowledge or a prophetic word for the listeners through song.

Transitioning into the flow can be challenging when worshippers aren't accustomed to it. The reason is that many singers think that if the music is still playing, then they're supposed to keep singing. However, with training, this can easily be overcome.

The flow itself is birthed out of the worshippers' relationship with God. When the lead worshippers are praying, studying their Bible, and spending time in the presence of God (outside of the worship service), that time spent will flow out of their spirit, bringing to life Ephesians 5:19 (NIV), *"speaking to one another with psalms, hymns, and songs from the Spirit. Sing and make music from your heart to the Lord,"*

One word of warning. The flow, or spontaneous worship, is not an opportunity for preaching worshippers to have a "mini-sermon" and take a text. God may move the worshippers to minister, but it will be in order. Remember that the role of the worshipper is the same as that of the cherubim who carries the Glory of the Lord. They go where the spirit says. Period!

9
PRACTICING HIS PRESENCE

As a recap, we have discussed being a skilled worker, an individual, and having a good work ethic. We talked about the importance of the worshipper/pastoral relationship and the sounds of the house. Finally, we briefly looked into a few different methods of worship.

Authoring this book has challenged me in every area I've discussed.

One important thing about all these areas is how vital they are to worship leaders *individually*. But even more essential is the unity of doing these things *corporately*.

Unless you are a one-man band with no accompanying instruments or singers, you will fall short of consistently attaining your objective of entering the Glory of God.

And that leads us into the next part of worship: *practicing His presence.*

One definition of a rehearsal is a "trial performance of a play or other work for later public performance." The key here is the first two words: trial performance. We often call this a practice session, meaning an "actual application or use of an idea, belief, or method as opposed to theories about such application or use."

However, the difference between rehearsing and practicing is a performance mindset versus an application mentality. As worship leaders, we have the stage. We have the mic. We have the attention of the audience. And we have been given a substantial chunk of time in the service. But if we are not careful, we can turn from worshippers into performers, and that's *not* God's intention for us as Lead Worshippers.

Why? Because quite honestly, when we become performers, the attention is no longer on God. It's on *us*.

As individuals within the worship experience, when we have handled our business up front, sought God in prayer and fasting, learned our music, learned our parts, learned the words, etc., all that is necessary is the corporate application of all that we've learned.

Ezekiel 1:9 KJV says, *"Their wings were joined one to another; they turned not when they went; they went every one straight forward."*

The purpose of practice is applying the methods we've discussed throughout this manual and not just reading about them, not just saying that we have a good idea, but putting those ideas in motion. For example, James 2:17 (MSG) says, *"Isn't it obvious that God-talk without God-acts is outrageous nonsense?"*

So, practicing His presence as a worship team is just that, taking time out of our busy schedules and devoting that time as a corporate body of worshippers to get into the presence of the Almighty while presenting Him with our gifts of worship in song. When we do that sincerely, God will show up. This now gives us a different expectation regarding leading the congregation into His presence because we've already been there together.

It's like getting in your car and going to the grocery store. Once you've gone there, it's easier to go there repeatedly. Then, when you need to take someone else there, you can show them the way to go because you've been where you're taking them.

I can't take you into a place of Glory if I've never been there. I, the lead worshipper, must find my way into that place. Then, I need to go there over and over. After that, the worship team and I will go there repeatedly. Now, *we* can lead the church into a place that *we* have been, and the cycle continues.

But it starts at home in my quiet, secret place.

I must establish an atmosphere of Glory in my house. You must Establish Glory in your home. Then we come together and set the atmosphere of Glory in the church *during practice*... Then, when it's time for service, we'll have no problem leading God's people into His Presence.

10
THE NEXT LEVEL OF PRAISE AND WORSHIP... THE GLORY

Earlier, I mentioned Benny Hinn and how his worship music changed my life when I realized how he found that path to Glory and has tapped in. The music itself may not always excite my flesh at all. We often go into services with the mindset of having a "good time." So, we sing three fast and two slow songs, then call that worship. Whether or not we say it out loud, we expect to see the people "get with us," lift their hands at the right moment, and even "shout."

For all of those who believe that this is it, I apologize. The Glory is *not* a physical experience. The Glory is not, "We had a good service today." The Glory is not, "We danced so hard that there was no preaching."

So, what is the Glory?

According to Wikipedia, "Glory" is one of the most frequently used words in scripture. In the Old Testament, the word is used to translate several Hebrew words, including *Hod* (הוד) and *kabod*; and in the New Testament, it is used to translate the Greek word *doxa* (δόξα). The Hebrew word *kabod* (K-B-D) originally means "weight" or "heaviness." The same word is used to express importance, honor, and majesty. Greek versions of the Hebrew Bible translated this concept with the word δόξα, which was then used extensively in the New Testament as well. *Doxa* originally meant "judgment, opinion," and by extension, "good reputation, honor."

Wikipedia, Webster's, and Google say a lot, but in short, the Glory is the presence of God as real as anything tangible.

The exciting part is that conditions need to be met for God to show Himself to us.

First, we must come prepared with our

sacrificial offerings. Leviticus 9 talks about how Moses called Aaron, his sons, and the elders, and he commanded them to bring various offerings to sacrifice before the Lord. Leviticus 9:6 says, "And Moses said, This is the thing which the Lord commanded that ye should do: and the glory of the Lord shall appear unto you."

Today, we no longer sacrifice calves, rams, lambs, and bulls. Instead, we surrender ourselves as *living* sacrifices.

Romans 12:1-2 (AMP) says it best:

Therefore I urge you, brothers and sisters, by the mercies of God, to present your bodies [dedicating all of yourselves, set apart] as a living sacrifice, holy and well-pleasing to God, which is your rational (logical, intelligent) act of worship. And do not be conformed to this world [any longer with its superficial values and customs], but be]transformed and progressively changed [as you mature spiritually] by the renewing of your mind [focusing on godly values and ethical attitudes], so that you may prove [for yourselves] what the will of God is, that which is good and acceptable and perfect [in His plan and purpose for you]."

Several parts of that scripture jump out at me. But I'll only briefly address two.

First, *"as a living sacrifice, holy and well-pleasing to God, which is"*—are you ready? Here it comes— "your rational, logical, intelligent act of worship." When we truly recognize *who God is*, it just makes sense that we should worship Him. It doesn't take a brain surgeon to understand this. So, here's a worship exercise I love that shows the greatness of God.

Sometimes, worship leaders will ask the congregation to think about one thing God has done for them and begin to worship Him for that one thing. We often see the congregation with glazed eyes, staring at the ceiling, looking for that *significant* thing God has done. The problem is that everyone assumes they must have something powerful in mind, life-altering, or a most unusual event.

What God showed me was to make worship simpler. We're always looking for that last, most fabulous thing He has done. But what about the little things? Do we worship Him for each breath that we take? So, let's say,

"Thank you, Lord, for the breath I just took." Now, you must say thank you again because you had to take another breath to say, "thank you." But when you say thank you for the third time, guess what? You just took another breath and are mandated by this exercise to thank Him again because you just took another breath. And this exercise is unending because you can never run out of reasons to thank God. Every time we give Him the fruit of our lips, He's given us another reason to worship Him...

Secondly, *"...that, you may prove for yourselves what the will of God is...."* How often have we worshiped with our stuff weighing on our hearts and minds? We pray and ask God to do this or that, take this away, give me that, handle this situation, change that person, move this mountain, but there's a song that says, "Give me you. Everything else can wait." If God's will be that we *"prosper and be in health, even as thy soul prospers"* (3 John 1:2,) why would we think He's not already fully aware of our issues? The key to success in the Kingdom is to handle His business, and He will handle ours. He's already given us the keys, but we need to prove that these keys unlock the door.

After we bring our sacrificial offerings, we must lay them at the altar. Leviticus 9:7 (MSG) says, *"Approach the Altar and sacrifice..."* your offerings. One part is going to the physical altar and casting your cares. All too often, we bring our sacrifices to the church, but we don't release them. Instead, we allow our concerns, issues, and problems to lead and guide us. In 1 Peter 5:7 TLB, we read, *"Let him have all your worries and cares, for he is always thinking about you and watching everything that concerns you."*

The other part is the altar of your heart, where the actual participation in the worship service itself comes into play. John 4:24 says, *"God is a Spirit: and they that worship him must worship him in spirit and in truth."* "In spirit" is from the heart. "In truth" is in Jesus (John 14:6, *"I am the way, the truth..."*. So, when we worship him in spirit and truth, in our hearts offering praise and honor, God sees His own reflection as the center of our lives. But to do that, we must participate in worship.

Participation isn't like the Blues Brothers, where the service is going on, and there's a light from heaven. Then, suddenly, they're doing cartwheels, flips, and spins down the aisle. Instead, participation is being *engaged* in worship. Sing, clap your hands, and even stand sometimes. Take in the entire worship experience. Allow the words of the songs to penetrate your heart and mind. Let the melodies resonate in your spirit. Don't fight it.

We've brought our sacrificial offerings and placed them on the altar. Now, we should expect that God will come, and we wait. Each time that Moses gave a command, in Leviticus 9, he ended that command with a promise: Lev 9:4 (KJV), *"...for today the Lord will appear unto you."* and Lev 9:6 (KJV), *"...the glory of the Lord shall appear unto you."* When we follow the process, a promise is fulfilled in the end.

Luke 24:49 (KJV) says, *"And, behold, I send the promise of my Father upon you: but tarry ye in the city of Jerusalem, until ye be endued with power from on high."* Jesus set their expectations. All they had to do was go there and wait.

Acts 2:1-3 (KJV), *"And when the day of*

Pentecost was fully come, they were all with one accord in one place. And suddenly there came a sound from heaven as of a rushing mighty wind, and it filled all the house where they were sitting. And there appeared to them cloven tongues like fire, and it sat upon each of them."

What makes this scripture pop is two words... *one accord*. Establishing Glory isn't just for the individual. The power comes in agreement and unity. Matthew 18:20 says, *"For where two or three are gathered together in my name, there am I in the midst of them."* When we share the Good News, we create an atmosphere of expectancy; this atmosphere is charged even higher when we raise our voices in unity, worshipping the Almighty God, the King of Kings, the Lord of Lords. We worship, watch, and wait *together,* expecting to receive power from on high.

This is what happens when a well-known evangelist comes to town. Believers come together from far and wide to be in the service. The environment is electrical. There's tension in the air. People are seeking a move of God, and they are waiting to see what's going to happen. The crazy part is that everyone in attendance is waiting for the same thing. They are seeking the same thing. So, it's only a matter of time before what they expect from God will come to pass.

Ezekiel 10:4: *"Then the glory of the LORD went up from the cherub, and stood over the threshold of the house, and the house was filled with the cloud, and the court was full of the brightness of the LORD'S glory."*

ACKNOWLEDGMENTS

I want to thank God for giving me this vision in writing. I pray every reader will be blessed tremendously. I'd also like to thank all the pastors, worship teams/choirs, and churches that endured the journey with me and helped me grow naturally, spiritually, and musically. I want to thank my friends and family for encouraging me to pursue what God has for me. Finally, I'd like to thank my wife for the prayers and understanding that God has put a fire in me that can only be subdued by long hours of praying, playing, and writing.

My love to you all!!

ABOUT THE AUTHOR

Jackie Smith, Jr. is an African-American writer who grew up in Columbus, Ohio. Using his experiences as a technical trainer, business owner, professional musician, and licensed minister he penned, Establishing Glory, a faith-based self-help series.

His goal in life is to help people be their best which he does it by shining an unfiltered light on the challenges of his own life including faith, marriage, music, divorce, and parenting in the 2000s.

facebook.com/MrJMerrill
twitter.com/MrJMerrill
instagram.com/MrJMerrill

www.ingramcontent.com/pod-product-compliance
Lightning Source LLC
Chambersburg PA
CBHW030100100526
44591CB00008B/210